FORESTRY COMMISSION GUIDE

THE NEW FORESTS
OF DARTMOOR

By

G. D. ROUSE, B.Sc.

Conservator of Forests for South West England
Forestry Commission

LONDON
HER MAJESTY'S STATIONERY OFFICE
1972

SBN 11 710034 X

Plate 1. Tall Douglas firs beside **Fernworthy Reservoir, near Chagford.**

Plate 2. The Old Devonport Leat, still carrying water from Two Bridges to Plymouth, seen in the Burrator Plantations.

Historical Introduction

Dartmoor Forest came into existence as a separate Royal Forest in 1204 when the rest of the county of Devon was disafforested. The boundaries of the Royal Forest were perambulated by twelve knights in 1240, and since that date they have not altered, though on passing from the royal ownership of Henry III to his brother Richard, Earl of Cornwall, technically it ceased to be a Royal Forest and became a chase. In those unsettled times, however, the forest reverted to the Crown and since 1337 it has been permanently annexed to the Duchy of Cornwall as an appanage of the Prince of Wales.

In the times of King Henry III a Royal Forest was not necessarily a tract of wild country densely stocked with trees, but, as Manwood defines it in his Forest Laws, "a certain territory of woody grounds

4

and fruitful pastures, privileged for wild beasts and fowls of Forest, Chase and Warren to rest and abide in, in the safe protection of the King, for his princely delight and pleasure".

From the fact that it was early bestowed upon Richard, Earl of Cornwall, the cynic might deduce that it was not one of those forests which afforded the greatest princely delight and pleasure. We can do no more than surmise here, but the distance from London and Winchester is great and the rainfall higher than any in the Kingdom except for limited parts of Snowdonia and the Lake District; frequent mists and the ubiquitous occurrence of granite boulders of all sizes would not add to the pleasures of hunting on horseback; but it may perhaps be that the poor nature of the woodlands did not supply shelter and browse for an adequate stock of red deer. However, red deer certainly did exist on Dartmoor for a jury at a Survey Court for the Forest of Dartmoor did present "that one Edwarde Ashe in the sommer tyme of 1607 was . . . (by his own confession) at the rowsinge of a stagge and was at huntinge of the same dere with hounds till he was kild about Blanchdon, wch. was

Plate 3. Prehistoric stone circle at Fernworthy.

5

Plate 4. Medieval clapper bridge at Postbridge.

not lawful to be donne without license". The same jury also found "that Willm Chastie (by his owne confessyon) kild a stagge wth a pece or gun . . . about Blacktorrebeare . . .".

Samuel Rowe, quoting Mrs. Bray, also reports that "Towards the end of the last (eighteenth) century Red Deer were very plentiful upon Dartmoor, so much so, that in consequence of the complaints of the farmers, they were exterminated by the staghounds of the Duke of Bedford, sent down from Woburn for the purpose. Tavistock was so glutted with venison that only the haunches of the animals killed were saved, the rest being given to the hounds".

Since the killing of the last indigenous deer in about 1780 there have been occasional reports of red deer, either singly or in small groups, on the fringes and less frequently in the centre of the Moor. There is a herd established at Lydford on the western fringes of the Moor from which some of the biggest stags recorded in this country have recently been shot.

From the earliest historical times tin was an important product

6

from Dartmoor, and the first method of exploitation was by working the gravel beds of the many streams and rivers flowing southward from the moor—an operation known as "streaming". Although the tin-miners used peat for fuel it is certain that they would have used wood in preference to peat as far as it was available, and very few records of sales of wood from within the boundaries of the forest exist: for instance, £40 was paid for 8 acres of underwood at Black Tors Beare probably about the year 1620, and in 1587 a man was fined 3d. at the Manor and Forest Court of Lydford North for the illegal felling of oaks in the same place.

So much for the existence of woods. On the other hand we need look no further than Grimspound and other prehistoric remains from Mesolithic to the Bronze Ages scattered widely throughout the moor for evidence of the extensive occupation of the area by peoples whose method of living and limited range of implements debarred them from living in primaeval forest.

Plate 5. Shelterbelts of beech around Archerton House, near Postbridge.

From the scanty evidence so far reviewed we may deduce that from prehistoric times Dartmoor Forest contained extensive tracts of open moorland. Such woodland as existed would probably be round the lower fringes of the moor with a few scattered small woods in the upper valleys on the more sheltered, warmer south and south-west facing slopes where drainage was good and peat absent. Until a systematic analysis of the peat bogs of the moor is carried out there is no reason to believe that any tree species other than oak, birch, alder, willow, rowan, hazel and holly were present.

The Weather on Dartmoor

When the sun shines Dartmoor is one of the most delightful areas of wild moorland and woodland scenery in southern Britain; but when the sky becomes overcast, grey and lowering the whole atmosphere changes, and there are few places in the whole of the country which can adopt a more sinister appearance. Rapid changes in the weather are one of the features of Dartmoor. The most publicised change is the sudden descent of thick impenetrable fogs, when the loneliness imposed almost without warning on the walker can be frightening.

The average rainfall for the centre of the moor is over 90 inches per year, and for much of the high ground it is over 80 inches. Compared with some mountainous areas of Wales and the west highlands of Scotland this amount of rainfall is not impressive, but once again it is the suddenness of change which causes the dramatic effect.

September 29th, 1960, was an ideal day for walking and picnicking on the moor, but that evening a storm broke and torrential rain fell throughout the night and carried on into the next morning. By midday on the next day all the rivers rising on the moor had burst their banks; many roads were flooded and even the main road bridges were declared unsafe because riverside trees had been washed away and built up dangerous barriers above the bridges against which they had been swept. At one time the only road open by which a traveller could get off the centre of the moor was that from Princetown to Yelverton.

Snow occurs on the moor in most years but does not usually lie long, but when it does lie, the isolation can be complete. Once there is a fair cover of snow the roads can be blocked for periods of days or even weeks without any further fall because the strong winds whip the snow off the open moor and pile up fresh drifts on the roads more quickly than they can be cleared. On Thursday,

8

Plate 6. Eroded by the storms of centuries, a granite outcrop on the summit of Bellever Tor.

December 27th, 1962, snow started to fall on the moor, and by the next day many of the roads were impassable to normal traffic and from then until March 1st, 1963, supplies to Bellever and even to Postbridge were intermittent and relied upon special transport from the Royal Marines, or an RAF helicopter or a 4-wheel drive Landrover towing an improvised sledge. Conditions finally returned to normal on March 7th. The moor dwellers have to be a hardy race to survive such winters, and those who lived through 1962/63 do not start the winter now with empty store cupboards.

Geology

The dominant geological feature of Dartmoor is the great central mass of granite which forms all the high ground. An interesting characteristic of this granite is its differential disintegration, some of

9

it breaking down easily to a coarse angular sandy gravel known locally as 'growan' whilst embedded in this matrix there remain huge boulders of hard granite often with rounded contours as if they had already been exposed to eons of weathering.

It is possible that some of the tors, consisting of huge boulders of granite which look as if they might have been thrown together by giants of a previous age, have come into being by the erosion of the growan through which the boulders were originally dispersed.

Another form of disintegration of the granite has been brought about by kaolinisation due to the action of fluorine vapour which has resulted in the valuable deposits of china clay occurring in commercial quantities round the southern fringes of the moor.

In addition to the tin mentioned earlier, there are lodes of ores containing copper, lead, arsenic, silver, wolfram, manganese and iron, the mining of which was once carried out extensively, but the mines have gradually closed. The last at Great Rock near Hennock closed in the 1960's.

Surrounding the granite on west, north and east are the Culm shales and clays of the Carboniferous period. These were deposited before the intrusion of the granite which caused the formation of a highly mineralised metamorphic aureole. The southern boundary of the granite is similarly fringed by beds of Devonian age.

History of Planting on the Moor

There is no record of any serious tree-planting on the moor until the time of the "improvers". Notable work was done by Sir Francis Buller at Prince Hall, and by Sir Thomas Tyrwhitt at Tor Royal.

The building of Tor Royal was completed in 1798 and throughout the first decade of the nineteenth century experimental planting of the greatest importance was undertaken primarily to form shelterbelts around the house and farm buildings and the adjacent newly cultivated fields. All this was done on a bare windswept plateau, only slightly sheltered from the prevailing south-westerly winds, at an elevation between 1,200 and 1,450 feet, with a choice of species limited to Scots pine, Norway spruce and European larch amongst the conifers and to oak, beech and sycamore as the only broadleaved species likely to survive the rigours of the local climate.

The Duchy of Cornwall extended the plantations on the moor by establishing a conifer plantation at Brimpts in 1862.

The benefits of shelter and the possibility of successful planting had been established on the inhospitable moor, and throughout the

Plate 7. The East Dart flows below the Bellever sprucewoods.

next half century various small clumps and shelterbelts were planted by the more progressive owners, but nothing on a large scale was undertaken.

It required the impetus of the 1914–18 war to bring about the next major development when, spurred on by the twin motives of replenishing the nation's devastated timber resources and alleviating the post-war unemployment in Plymouth, the Prince of Wales and his advisers conceived, in the immediate post-war years, the scheme of planting up 5,000 acres on the moor.

Before embarking on this ambitious project the Duchy consulted Mr. C. O. Hanson, the regional officer of the Forestry Commission, who produced a detailed plan which relied to a considerable extent upon the relatively newly-introduced Sitka spruce.

From the outset the Duchy had clearly in mind that, in addition to the two primary objectives already mentioned, the scheme would confer substantial benefits upon the farmers and commoners on the moor by giving much-needed shelter and also by developing a road

Plate 8. Felling a Sitka spruce at Fernworthy.

Plate 9. Loading saw-logs at Bellever, using a lorry-mounted hydraulic hoist.

system which would be needed for the extraction of timber; and it was also considered possible that when the new woodland came into full production the extension of the railway from Princetown or Moretonhampstead would be justified.

The programme was tackled energetically and by 1930 some 1,200 acres had been established, mainly at Fernworthy with smaller woods at Frenchbeer, Beardown, Brimps and Bellever. In 1930, however, these areas together with other extensive areas at Bellever were sold to the Forestry Commission, and at the same time Torquay Corporation constructed a weir and intake on the headwaters of the South Teign river at Fernworthy. The present reservoir was not completed until 1942.

A little planting, mainly with Norway spruce, was done in 1931 immediately to the south of Bellever; but the main work of that season consisted of repairing the ravages caused by sheep and ponies browsing in the outlying plantations. This replacement of failures after an interval of ten years since the original planting resulted in

Plate 10. An overhead skyline carriage, operated by a winch on a tractor, draws a log to the roadside at Bellever.

14

the development of a two-storied high forest in parts of Brimpts and Beardown. This was particularly noteworthy at Beardown where the younger trees rapidly occupied the top storey. Here the more sheltered ground to the south east of the Devonport Leat had originally been planted with Douglas fir much of which had survived but had not flourished. Profiting by the experience gained by the Duchy during ten years of extensive planting, the Forestry Commission restocked the Douglas fir with Sitka spruce which are ideally suited to the site, and, soon towering head and shoulders above their weaker neighbours, the widely-spaced Sitka were able to develop with almost unrestricted crowns, so that, after only thirty-two years of growth, the largest Sitka had a girth at breast height of over five feet whilst the biggest Douglas, although ten years older, did not exceed three feet. The Sitka spruce, however, suffered for their uncontrolled vigour by becoming heavily and coarsely branched; the resultant rough plantation has been felled and the land replanted.

By 1935 the remainder of Brimpts had been planted, and by 1938 the eastern slopes of Bellever Tor and Lakehead Hill had been completed. During the war of 1939–45 work was drastically curtailed by shortage of labour, but the western slopes of Bellever and Lakehead were planted between 1940 and 1943. A short burst of intensive activity after the war completed the programme: the whole of Soussons Down, which was leased from the Duchy in 1945, was planted between 1947 and 1949, and Beardown was completed in 1950.

The Duchy planting at Fernworthy had been concentrated in two blocks separated by the valley of the South Teign River, and the upper limit of planting had been drawn at approximately the 1,500 foot contour. In the decade before the war the Forestry Commission planted the boulder-strewn valley of the South Teign up to the Hemstone Rocks; and finally in 1950 and 1951, with the heavier mechanical equipment for ploughing and the generally improved techniques which had by then been developed, the exposed tops above 1,500 feet, and rising to 1,650 feet, were planted with Sitka spruce.

This virtually completed the planting of all the areas available to the Forestry Commission within the bounds of the Royal Forest of Dartmoor, a total of almost 3,200 acres—by no means a small achievement, and yet almost 2,000 acres short of the target originally set by the Prince of Wales and so widely approved in 1920. The extent of these properties is shown on the map on the centre pages.

Other Developments

Those who knew and frequented the moor during the Middle Ages were very few in number. After it had ceased to provide "princely delight and pleasure" for the King, the moor was for centuries known only to those few who wrested a meagre living from it: the ancient tenement holders, the graziers, the tin-miners, and those hardy travellers who used the shortest routes between the big ecclesiastical houses which had been established round the southern fringes of the moor.

In 1771 a Bill was introduced into Parliament to authorise the construction of a road from Moretonhampstead to Tavistock across the centre of the moor. Opposition to this proposal was based solely on the argument that the road would divert trade from places along the existing highway skirting the moor, and it was not until 1792 that a road, backed by the powerful influence of the Duke of Bedford who held extensive estates round Tavistock, was finally constructed.

Plate 11. A lorry takes up its load of pit props from the Burrator larchwoods.

Plate 12. A thinned plantation of Sitka spruce at Fernworthy. The better trees survive to grow larger after this harvest of poles and saw-logs.

17

Plate 13. Trimming-off the branches from felled spruce trees, using power saws.

The accommodation of prisoners from the Napoleonic wars was the reason for the establishment of the prison at the site named Princetown by Sir Thomas Tyrwhitt after his friend, the Prince of Wales. The servicing of the prison resulted in the development of a small thriving township dependent upon, and to a large extent built by, the prisoners.

Prisoners on extended parole were permitted to build homes for themselves within a wide radius of Princetown and were encouraged to supplement their slender rations by raising such foodstuff as they could. One of these small homesteads was built on the east bank of the East Dart about a mile south of Bellever Bridge. Here the Frenchmen supplemented their diet by introducing their native large edible snail which became acclimatised and thrived there.

The ruins of this house, marked on the 6-inch Ordnance Survey map as Snaily House, are enveloped in the Forestry Commission's spruce plantations, and although the men who planted the area in 1935 found a few large white snails in the vicinity, none have recently been observed and it may be presumed that the dense spruce thicket has made it no longer a suitable habitat for this snail.

With the ending of the Napoleonic Wars the prison fell into disuse and it seemed that unemployment would cause Princetown to become deserted until, in 1850, the prison became a civil penitentiary.

Even in 1920 the main interest in Dartmoor was that of the Duchy of Cornwall acting as good landlords concerned to improve the standard of living of their tenants and other small communities isolated in the moor; but the opening of the road from Moretonhampstead to Tavistock and the subsequent establishment of the scattered hamlet of Postbridge had opened up the moor to a new kind of visitor—the botanist and archaeologist. The archaeologists found the moor to be a fruitful area for their pioneer investigations since it is widely scattered with prehistoric pounds, hut-circles and burial chambers, the latter frequently described as "kistvaens", from the Celtic *cist vaen* or stone chest. The hut-circles left little scope for research since the walls are built of massive granite rocks to a

Plate 14. Turning a log with a cant-hook, so that all sides can be trimmed.

19

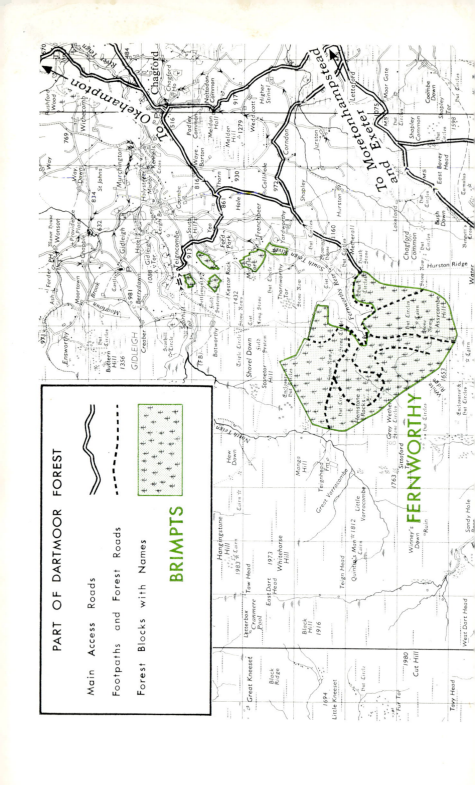

PART OF DARTMOOR FOREST

Main Access Roads

Footpaths and Forest Roads

Forest Blocks with Names

BRIMPTS

FERNWORTHY

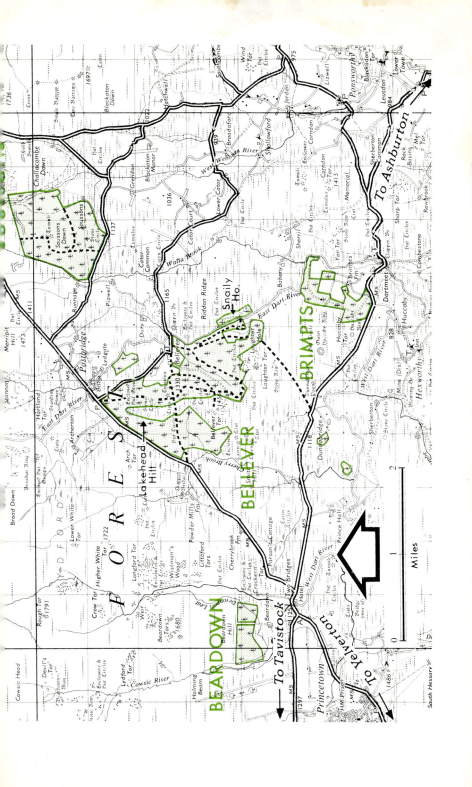

Plate 15. Measuring a log, and cross-cutting a ten-foot length with the power-saw.

height of some two or three feet only, but the kistvaens consist of a small burial chamber totally enclosed by natural granite blocks and then covered by a small mound of earth and peat. In an era when archaeology had not been developed into a science the great majority of these chambers were opened up in a search for bones, or utensils and ornaments which might have been buried with the dead: in the process, the granite stones were rolled or levered out of the way where they continue to lie in any form of disorder, except for those few cases where the more scrupulous investigators made some scant effort to replace the stones approximately as they found them. In many instances, however, these remnants of prehistoric occupants of the moor have been unwittingly destroyed by local farmers and graziers who required stone for walls or gate posts and took the nearest pieces suitable for their purpose.

During the period 1920–1930 many sites of this nature were planted over at Fernworthy, although the distinguishable features of hut-circles, stone-rows and stone-circles were sedulously preserved.

Plate 16. Loading poles on to a trailer, using a tractor-mounted hydraulic hoist.

Various factors, including the improvement of the roads on the moor, the increased reliability of motor transport and longer paid holidays, resulted in larger numbers of visitors reaching the moor in the decade before the last war. The realisation grew that the moor was of value not only as a means of earning a livelihood for the hardy race of moor-dwellers but also as one of the few remaining wide open spaces in the south of England where a large section of the population may seek recreation during the short months of summer.

It was not unnatural therefore that, in the atmosphere that was prevailing at that time, the Council for the Preservation of Rural England approached the Forestry Commission in 1934 with a request that certain areas within the bounds sold to the Commission by the Duchy should remain un-forested mainly to preserve certain vistas but also to ensure that some prehistoric features should not be further disturbed. As a result of the ensuing negotiations an informal agreement was reached to the effect that no planting would be done on some 250 acres without prior consultation

Plate 17. The quaint distorted oaks of Wistman's Wood, hung with epiphytic lichens, ferns and mosses.

with the C.P.R.E. It is interesting and instructive to review the situation now that nearly forty years have passed since this decision was reached. During that time the trees closely surrounding the hut-circles and stone-rows at Fernworthy have grown up and closed over, so that all vegetation has been suppressed and the stones stand out clearly amongst a fine carpet of fallen needles. By contrast the pound and hut-circles on the reserved land at Lakehead are difficult to discern due to the rank growth of heather, willow, bramble, rushes and purple moor grass.

Most of the plantations formed before the war have grown up so that they no longer show the straight black lines of their first formation: instead they clothe the hills with varying shades of green which form a pleasant contrast to the heathy colours of the open moor and the bright green of the cultivated pastures. The woods are now an integral part of the beauty of the moor and enhance the scenery. There is clearly scope for some further increase in the extent of the woodlands in carefully chosen sites. Change in itself has now been clearly shown to remain completely compatible with the preservation of this grand and ancient forest: but now it will be for the delight and pleasure of the people instead of solely for the sport of kings and princes.

Dartmoor National Park

In the decade before the war the Forestry Commission took practical steps to meet the increasing needs of the population for large tracts of wild country to be put at their disposal for recreational purposes by establishing Forest Parks, the first such Forest Park being that of Argyll, created by the Forestry Commission with the co-operation of Glasgow Corporation in 1936. Other Forest Parks in Wales and England followed shortly afterwards; Snowdonia in 1937 and the Forest of Dean in 1938; and several others have since been established.

Dartmoor was not suitable for this purpose because the Forestry Commission's holding of land was relatively insignificant and the three major blocks of forest were separated by open moorland and enclosed pastures held in other ownerships.

In 1949 the requirements of the public for open recreational spaces were given more formal acknowledgment by the passing of the National Parks and Access to the Countryside Act. This very extensive and comprehensive Act provided for the establishment of

Plate 18. Oakwoods beside the River Meavy, near Yelverton.

a National Parks Commission charged with the duty of preserving and enhancing the natural beauty in England and Wales, particularly in those areas to be designated as National Parks. In addition, the Act lays upon the National Parks Commission (now the Countryside Commission), the Nature Conservancy and the local authorities the duty to pay due regard to the needs of agriculture and forestry.

Dartmoor National Park was created in 1951, with its boundaries extending well beyond those of the ancient Royal Forest of Dartmoor and the adjacent open moorland and commons. As shown on the map at the end of this booklet, the new Park embraces some 365 square miles bounded approximately on the north and west by the main road from Exeter to Tavistock via Okehampton, A30 and A386; on the east by a stretch of the River Teign; on the south east by the main road (A38) from Exeter to Plymouth, passing through Ashburton, Buckfastleigh and Ivybridge; and on the south west by minor roads from Ivybridge joining A386 again a short distance south of Yelverton.

There are many demands upon the limited area of the National Park, and fears have been expressed that uncontrolled afforestation might upset the balance of land use. In consequence the Forestry

Commission, in consultation with the Timber Growers' Organisation and the Country Landowners' Association, have negotiated an agreement with the Dartmoor National Park Committee, which consulted the appropriate amenity societies. This agreement divides the whole area of the Park into three zones as follows:

(*a*) areas where there is a strong presumption that afforestation would be acceptable:—5,271 acres;

(*b*) intermediate areas which in the long term may be subject to reviews, and in the short term may admit afforestation proposals of acceptable scale and character in the particular locality:—113,950 acres;

(*c*) areas where there is a strong presumption against afforestation:—114,379 acres.

Plate 19. Near Dartmeet the water-worn boulders of the turbulent East Dart are crossed by two bridges, the old broken clapper bridge (foreground) and the modern stone arches.

25

Plate 20. Dartmeet, where the East Dart, with its storm swept willows, is joined by the West Dart flowing in from the right.

Woodlands within the National Park

The high ground and open moorland of Dartmoor contains the sources of many streams and rivers which at first flow in relatively shallow valleys across the hard granite surface of the moor. On leaving the granite boss, however, these turbulent rivers have carved for themselves deep valleys and gorges through the softer surrounding rocks of the Culm and Upper Devonian Measures. These steep-sided valleys are unsuitable for agriculture, but, at a lower elevation than the moor and with a deeper and more fertile soil, except where the process of erosion has left hard projections of bare rock, they are well suited to the growth of trees.

In the centuries of civilisation before the advent of the bulldozer, transport was extremely difficult in these valleys and in many places it was limited to the sure-footed mule, the pack-horse and the slow plodding oxen. Although the sites may have been suitable for it, the

26

growth of heavy timber was therefore not practised since it could not be transported to distant markets. However the rural communities were to a large extent self-supporting and the woodlands had an important part to play in the economy.

Oak coppice was the most valuable crop: from its bark, which could conveniently be carried off the steep hillsides by pack-horse, tannin was extracted, which in turn was used in the production of leather from the hides of the farm stock. Bark-stripping provided useful employment for women and children. The coppice poles from which the bark had been removed were converted, on roughly levelled hearths on the hill side, to charcoal, which, again, was easily removed by pack-horse. A small proportion of the poles was used locally for fuel, for the maintenance of stockfencing and for repairs to agricultural buildings, whilst a small amount of timber near the homesteads was allowed to grow on to large size to provide more permanent shelter for the farm and, ultimately, constructional timber.

Plate 21. A clearing in the Fernworthy woods, replanted with young Sitka spruce trees.

Plate 22. The two bridges at Bellever: The old, broken clapper bridge, with the three graceful granite arches of the modern road bridge beyond.

The nineteenth century and the first decades of the twentieth century saw the breakdown of this close integration of the woodlands with the whole rural economy. Coal transported from Tyneside and South Wales by small coastal vessels to the many harbours and beaches never far from the fringes of Dartmoor, replaced charcoal as a fuel; and tanning materials were produced more cheaply from newly-developing tropical countries and, later, were supplemented by artificial chemicals; thus the oak woods were allowed to fall into disuse.

However there was an increasing interest in the growing of trees not only for their utility but also for the improvement which they could make on the scenery of a barren landscape, and Rowe, in his "Perambulations of the Antient and Royal Forest of Dartmoor" records that his route "will take us immediately below Auswell Rocks, and through a succession of fine woods and plantations belonging to Mr. Baldwin J. P. Bastard of Buckland Court, with Holne Chase full in view on the opposite side of the Dart. The

28

ancestor of the present owner—the late Col. Bastard—early in the century purchased Auswell Manor, and planted the waste land with fir, larch, and other forest trees, on so extensive a scale that the thanks of the House of Commons were given him for what was designated, his patriotism''.

Although there were a few other enlightened owners like Colonel Bastard who had introduced conifers into their woodlands, at the outbreak of war in 1939 the great majority of the woods in the valleys of the Okement, Taw, Teign, Bovey, Dart, Avon, Erme, Yealm, Plym, Meavy, Walkham, Tavy and Lyd—all rivers rising on the moor—consisted of oak coppice in varying stages of dereliction. During the war of 1939–45 the most accessible woods were cut over to provide mining timber for South Wales, charcoal and a little poor sawmill timber, and this additional felling served to emphasise the great need for the rehabilitation of these derelict woodlands into something far better after the war was over.

Two motives impelled several private owners to undertake this work. One of these motives envisaged well-managed productive woodlands as a means of giving healthful employment in rural surroundings, increasing the standard of living of those who already lived in the country, and reversing the drift from the land to the city, whilst at the same time making the best use of limited land resources by carefully combining the interests of agriculture and forestry. By this means a natural landscape would be built up truly reflecting the characteristics of the locality, each part having a nature and a beauty of its own.

The other motive is primarily financial though it is likely to lead to just the same benefits to the rural economics of Dartmoor and if wisely guided can develop in a manner wholly to safeguard the more intangible amenities of the district, whilst at the same time supplying much needed timber.

Wood is needed for the clay mines of Devon and the tin mines of Cornwall, as well as for more distant markets. The thinnings from the plantations are sold for making paper pulp, manufactured wallboards, woven sawn fencing, boxes, packing cases, pallets, shuttering, and many other uses. Over one quarter of the total current output, mainly from larger-sized thinnings and from clear fellings, is timber suitable for house-building.

Dartmoor has for upwards of three centuries been a source of pure water for the population which has grown up round its fringes. Pride of place for initiative in this respect must go to the City of Plymouth, for in 1591 Sir Francis Drake completed the leat which conducted the waters of the River Meavy to Plymouth. In 1793 the Company of Proprietors of the Plymouth Dock Waterworks undertook an even more ambitious scheme by bringing water in an open leat, now known as the Devonport Leat, from the West Dart, Cowsic and Blackabrook streams. When these leats proved to be insufficient to meet the growing demands for water, impounding reservoirs were built and, in order to protect the purity of supplies from the surrounding catchment areas, extensive plantations were formed. The most important of these within the National Park are Plymouth's reservoir and plantations at Burrator, and those of Torquay at Fernworthy and between Hennock (north-west of Chudleigh) and Moretonhampstead, where planting was started as early as 1899, though smaller undertakings such as that of Paignton on Holne Moor make their contribution to the scenery.

During the Ice Ages Dartmoor was never covered by a continuous ice sheet and in consequence no basins were gouged out by the grinding action of ice, and the moor is therefore devoid of any

Plate 23. Modern houses for Forest Workers at the hamlet of Bellever.

Plate 24. When the growth of spruce slackened in Soussons Plantation, phosphatic fertilisers were applied effectively from the air.

natural expanses of water. The lakes formed by impounding natural streams thus provide a welcome additional feature to the landscape whose beauty is enhanced by the surrounding trees.

The Forestry Commission's Contribution to Local Prosperity

The Forestry Commission now manages more than 4,700 acres of land within the National Park; of this nearly 2,500 acres are yielding supplies of timber, mainly from the operation of thinning out the crop and also from clear fellings of small areas which have reached maturity. As each year passes more and more plantations come into production. In the year 1970, 6,700 cubic metres (equal to about 6,700 tons) of timber was produced, and it is estimated that by the end of the century, when all the forest area is in full production, the annual out-turn of timber will be approaching 25,000 cubic metres

Plate 25. Fernworthy Reservoir.

(25,000 tons). Some measure of the work which this entails may be obtained from the fact that for every cubic metre of timber despatched from the forest about £3·50 will be paid for felling, trimming out, cross-cutting to lengths, extraction to roadside, bark peeling where required, and loading on to transport together with such ancillary payments as holiday pay.

New roads have been built mainly from rock and gravel quarried in the forests; existing roads, fences and drains have to be kept in repair; the areas which are clear felled at rotation age, now amounting to 40 acres per annum and rising to 90 acres by the end of the century, have to be replanted, and the whole forest protected against fire. From all this work the local economy benefits by some £40,000 annually. By the end of the century, in the unlikely event of prices remaining unchanged, this sum will rise to £150,000.

To provide for the workers needed in the forest ten new houses have been built in a small community at Bellever, 1¼ miles south of Postbridge, the road to which has recently become a public one maintainable by the County authorities.

The forests provide a national financial asset; they provide employment and homes in a healthy but rigorous rural climate; but they do more than this: they form an integral part of the beauty of Dartmoor National Park and in them at all times—except occasionally in conditions of extreme fire danger—the public are invited to enjoy the peaceful recreation of walking amid the tall and stately trees. Even those men of sterner stuff who march in the teeth of the gales and the rain from one windswept rocky tor to the next are often glad to turn aside for a period of peaceful solace in the deep woods whilst the tree tops sway and make their music in the wind a hundred feet above their heads.

Private Forestry

Private woodlands are mostly concentrated in the more sheltered valleys leading from the moor. They range in size from the extensive

Plate 26. Beech shelterbelt fringing the road to Prince Hall.

voods reaching for nearly five miles along the steep slopes above the iver Teign north of Moretonhampstead, to small understocked roups of trees providing shelter and a little early grazing for cattle. No complete inventory of all these woods has been made, but the otal exceeds 16,000 acres; roughly half of this is under systematic management for the production of timber.

Much of the work in these woods is more recent than that of the Forestry Commission and yields from them are therefore not yet so great; but in the course of time there is every reason to believe that their total production will outstrip that of the Commission. About 100 men are at present employed and more will be required as these young woods advance to maturity.

When new plantations are formed on open moorland it is inevitable that the straight rows of young conifers should stand out rather starkly against their surroundings, but experience has already shown at Fernworthy, Brimpts, Tottiford and Burrator that this is merely a passing phase whose duration is brief compared with the lifetime of the forest.

Plate 27. Burrator Reservoir with plantations on the slopes below Sharpitor.

In the wooded valleys, however, even this brief period of ado‑
lescence can be masked from view because a light screen of th
natural coppice or birch can be preserved so that the young tree
are brought up beneath the dappled shade which is only gradually
removed as the new crop develops to take its place.

The General Effect of Woodlands in the Park

The area of woodlands within the Dartmoor National Park is about
20,000 acres which is less than one tenth of the total area of the
Park; yet, because of the positions they occupy in relation to the
roads approaching the moor, they assume an importance in the
scenery greater than this ratio implies.

Plate 28. Brimpts Plantation near Dartmeet: spruce, Scots pine and beech.

One of the most attractive features of Dartmoor is the contrast between the serene permanence of solid granite tors and the constant change of scenery as sunlight follows the shadows of the fast-moving clouds and as each bend of the tortuous road opens out fresh and unexpected vistas.

The woodlands reflect and accentuate this contrast. Dominated by the tors and rugged escarpments and bounded by the boisterous brooks the forests themselves are permanent and yet within them there is constant change. Trees may grow up until they obscure a well-known view, but compensation is quickly gained by the felling of a small mature group opening up a new vista elsewhere. A dense impenetrable plantation is gradually opened out by successive thinnings until the enchanting glimpses of distant scenes between the swelling boles and spreading crowns tempt the traveller to leave the road and explore for himself the quiet fastnesses of the forest—a quietness disturbed at times by the rhythmic whirr of a saw and the staccato blow of an axe reminding him that among this broad expanse of moorland the woods provide a livelihood for men no less sturdy than those who peopled it before history began.

Acknowledgments

The cover picture was drawn by Colin Gibson, and is based on a photo taken by the Dart at Bellever by R. W. Genever. The maps are based, with permission, on Ordnance Survey one-inch and quarter-inch sheets; details were added by Marc Sale. The photographs are by H. L. Edlin, with the exceptions of Plates 5 and 26 by F. Collins, Plate 17 by Heather Angel, Plate 18 by G. D. Rouse, and Plate 24 by the *Western Morning News*.

Plate 29. Spring sunshine in the Burrator oakwoods.

Printed in England for Her Majesty's Stationery Office
by Wells KPL, Swindon Press, Swindon, Wilts.

Dd. 507132   K64   5/72